Heroes of the Old Testament
Bible Story Mazes

Written by Kim Rankin

Illustrated by Vanessa Filkins

Cover by Vanessa Filkins

Shining Star Publications, Copyright © 1992
A Division of Good Apple

ISBN No. 0-86653-710-4

Standard Subject Code TA ac

Printing No. 98765432

Shining Star Publications
23740 Hawthorne Boulevard
Torrance, CA 90505-5927
A Division of Frank Schaffer Publications, Inc.

Unless otherwise indicated, the New International Version of the Bible was used in preparing the activities in this book.

Table of Contents

Shining Star Publications, Copyright © 1992, A division of Good Apple   SS2846

To Parents and Teachers

The twenty Bible stories and mazes in this book will challenge every young mind. The short Bible-based stories give an excellent overview of important stories from Genesis to Jonah. Each story includes a challenge, a maze, and Scripture references so the children can follow up with additional Scripture study. The New International Version of the Bible is used for all Scripture quotations.

The mazes and stories can be used with individuals, small groups, classes, and large groups at parties. Here are a few ways to use them:

1. Give the book to individual children and let them read and complete the mazes on their own. Small children will need assistance.

2. In the classroom setting the stories may be read to nonreaders or beginning readers, while older children can read the stories for themselves. The challenges and mazes can serve as follow-up activities.

3. Reproduce enough mazes and stories for each member of your group and encourage each child to assemble his/her own book of stories and mazes.

4. If a time limit is given, the mazes make good party games to determine who can get through the mazes first.

5. After children read or hear the story, give them an appropriate memory verse from Scripture references at the beginning of the story. When they know memory verses, they receive awards for good work.

6. Use the mazes in a learning center or at a learning table. Laminate or cover the maze with clear adhesive plastic. Children can use crayons to mark the answers. The answers can be rubbed off with a tissue, and the maze can be used again by other students.

Any way you choose to use the stories and mazes in this book, the children are sure to enjoy and learn from the experience. The challenging mazes are guaranteed to provide hours of delightful learning for children ages 5-11.

Adam

Genesis 1:1-31; 2:1-3

"In the beginning God created the heavens and the earth. Now the earth was formless and empty, darkness was over the surface of the deep, and the Spirit of God was hovering over the waters." On the first day, God said, "Let there be light," and there was light. On the second day, God said, "Let there be an expanse between the waters to separate water from water," and He called it "sky." On the third day, God said, "Let the water under the sky be gathered to one place, and let dry ground appear." On the fourth day, God said, "Let there be lights in the expanse of the sky to separate the day from the night, and let them serve as signs to mark seasons and days and years, and let them be lights in the expanse of the sky to give light on the earth." On the fifth day, God said, "Let the water teem with living creatures, and let birds fly above the earth across the expanse of the sky." God blessed them and said, "Be fruitful and increase in number and fill the water in the seas, and let the birds increase on the earth." On the sixth day, God said, "Let the land produce living creatures according to their kinds: livestock, creatures that move along the ground, and wild animals, each according to its kind." Then God created man in His own image, to rule over the earth and over all the creatures on the earth, and named him Adam. By the seventh day, God had finished His work. He blessed the day and made it holy, and He rested from all His work.

Challenge:

On the first day God said, "Let there be light." Help the sun's rays find their way to the earth.

Shining Star Publications, Copyright © 1992, A division of Good Apple

Eve

Genesis 2:8, 15-23; 3:6

God had made the Garden of Eden, and He put Adam there to care for it. God told Adam, "You are free to eat from any tree in the garden; but you must not eat from the tree of the knowledge of good and evil, for when you eat of it you will surely die."

"Now the Lord God had formed out of the ground all the beasts of the field and all the birds of the air." He brought the animals and the birds to Adam. Adam gave names to all the living creatures.

God saw that the man needed a suitable helper, so He caused Adam to fall into a deep sleep. God took one of Adam's ribs and made a woman from the rib. God brought her to Adam. Adam said, "This is now bone of my bones and flesh of my flesh; she shall be called 'woman,' for she was taken out of man." One day Eve disobeyed God and ate fruit from the tree of the knowledge of good and evil. Then she gave some to Adam. That was the beginning of sin on earth.

Challenge:

Can you find your way through the leaves and to the seed inside the fruit?

SS2846

Noah

Genesis 6-9:17

Men and women began to increase in number on the earth. When the Lord saw all the wickedness and evil that was going on, His heart filled with pain. He said, " 'I will wipe mankind, whom I have created, from the face of the earth—men and animals, and creatures that move along the ground, and birds of the air—for I am grieved that I have made them.' But Noah found favor in the eyes of the Lord."

Noah was a righteous man. He had three sons: Shem, Ham and Japheth. God told Noah and his sons to build an ark, for He was going to send a great flood to destroy all life on the earth. When the ark was finished, Noah and his sons were to gather two of every animal, male and female, and put them in the ark.

When all of God's instructions had been carried out, He said to Noah, "Go into the ark, you and your whole family, because I have found you righteous in this generation." Then the Lord shut the door. It rained for forty days and forty nights until the whole earth was flooded.

God remembered Noah and his family. He sent a wind over the earth to dry up the water. Noah opened the window and sent out a dove. It returned because there was water over all the surface of the earth. Noah waited and then sent the dove out again. It returned with an olive leaf. Noah knew the waters had receded. When the ground had dried, God said to Noah, "Come out of the ark, you and your wife and your sons and their wives. Bring out every kind of living creature that is with you–the birds, the animals, and all the creatures that move along the ground–so they can multiply on the earth and be fruitful and increase in number upon it." God promised that He would never again destroy the earth with water. He put a rainbow in the sky as a sign of the covenant between God and all living creatures on the earth.

Challenge:

Draw a line to help Noah find the rest of the animals inside the ark.

Abraham

Genesis 12; 15; 17

God told Abram, "Leave your country, your people and your father's household and go to the land I will show you. I will make you into a great nation and I will bless you; I will make your name great, and you will be a blessing. I will bless those who bless you, and whoever curses you I will curse; and all peoples on earth will be blessed through you." So Abram left for Canaan, as the Lord had told him.

After may years, Abram began to wonder how God would make him the father of nations. Abram said, "O Sovereign Lord, what can you give me since I remain childless and the one who will inherit my estate is Eliezer of Damascus? " Then the Lord came to him and said, "Look up at the heavens and count the stars.... So shall your offspring be."

"When Abram was ninety-nine years old, the Lord appeared to him and said, 'I am God Almighty; walk before me and be blameless. I will confirm my covenant between me and you and will greatly increase your numbers.' " God told Abram, "...your name will be Abraham, for I have made you a father of many nations." He also said, "As for Sarai your wife, you are no longer to call her Sarai, her name will be Sarah.... I will bless her so that she will be the mother of nations; kings of peoples will come from her." Abraham fell facedown, laughed, and said to himself, "Will a son be born to a man a hundred years old? Will Sarah bear a child at the age of ninety?" Then God said to Abraham, "Yes, but your wife Sarah will bear you a son, and you will call him Isaac."

Challenge:

Help Abraham and Sarah find the Promised Land.

SS2846

The Promised Land

11

Isaac and Rebekah

Genesis 24

Abraham was getting old, but his son Isaac was still unmarried. Abraham sent his chief servant to Canaan to find a wife for Isaac. The servant took ten of his master's camels and all kinds of good things from his master. He made his way to the town of Nahor. There, he rested his camels by a well outside the town. He prayed to the Lord, that he would find the right woman for Isaac. No sooner had he finished praying, when a woman came to get water from the well. The servant went to her and asked for a drink. She gave him a drink and then drew water for his camels until they were filled. He asked her name, and gave her two bracelets and a ring of gold. She said her name was Rebekah, the daughter of Bethuel, the son that Milcah bore to Nahor.

Rebekah took him to her father. Abraham's servant told her father that he had come to ask for Rebekah's hand in marriage for his master's son Isaac. The next morning, Abraham's servant started for home with Rebekah. When they arrived back in Canaan, Isaac ran up to greet them. Rebekah became Isaac's wife, and he loved her.

Challenge:

Help the servant find a wife for Isaac.

SS2846

Jacob

Genesis 28-29

Jacob's father, Isaac, called for him. Isaac said to Jacob, "Do not marry a Canaanite woman. Go at once to Paddan Aram, to the house of your mother's father Bethuel. Take a wife for yourself there, from among the daughters of Laban, your mother's brother. May God Almighty bless you and make you fruitful and increase your numbers until you become a community of peoples." Then Jacob left to go to his uncle's home.

One night on his journey, Jacob had a dream. He saw a stairway resting on the earth with its top reaching the heavens. Angels were climbing up and down on it. At the top, stood the Lord who said, "I am the Lord, the God of your father Abraham and the God of Isaac. I will give you and your descendants the land on which you are lying. Your descendants will be like the dust of the earth, and you will spread out to the west and to the east, to the north and to the south. All peoples on earth will be blessed through you and your offspring." The next morning Jacob vowed, "If God will be with me and will watch over me on this journey I am taking and will give me food to eat and clothes to wear so that I return safely to my father's house, then the Lord will be my God...." Jacob continued his journey until he reached Laban's home, where he stayed for awhile.

One day Laban said to Jacob, "Just because you are a relative of mine, should you work for me for nothing?" Jacob answered, "I'll work for you seven years in return for your younger daughter Rachel." Jacob worked for seven years and then asked for Rachel. Laban brought together all the people of the place and gave a feast. When evening came, he took his oldest daughter Leah and gave her to Jacob. Jacob asked Laban, "...I served you for Rachel, didn't I? Why have you deceived me?" Laban agreed to give Rachel to Jacob for another seven years work. Jacob agreed, and Rachel became his wife.

Challenge:

Can you help Jacob find the stairs, food, clothes, older sister Leah, and finally Rachel.

SS2846

stairs

food

clothes

Rachel

Leah

15

SS2846

Joseph

Genesis 37; 39; 41; 42

Jacob had many sons, but he loved Joseph the most. He made Joseph a robe of many colors. When the other brothers saw that their father loved him more than any of them, they hated Joseph and could not speak a kind word to him. Then Joseph had a dream that someday his brothers would serve him. When he told it to his brothers, they hated him even more. One day they sold him to some Midianite merchants on their way to Egypt. The brothers dipped Joseph's coat in the blood of an animal. They went home and told Jacob that Joseph had been killed by a wild beast. Joseph's father mourned for days.

In Egypt, Joseph was sold as a slave and worked without pay in Potiphar's house. Potiphar was a captain in the army of the king of Egypt, and was a rich and important man. Joseph was a good worker and everyone liked him—everyone except Potiphar's wife! She told lies about him and because of her lies, Joseph was sent to prison.

God gave Joseph a special talent—he could tell people what their dreams meant. After the word was out that Joseph could interpret dreams, Pharaoh, the king of Egypt, called for Joseph to explain a dream that had been troubling him. Joseph told Pharaoh, "Seven years of great abundance are coming throughout the land of Egypt, but seven years of famine will follow them. Then all the abundance in Egypt will be forgotten, and the famine will ravage the land. The abundance in the land will not be remembered, because the famine that follows it will be so severe." Pharaoh believed Joseph. He told Joseph that he was putting him in charge of the land of Egypt. Joseph became a very important man in Egypt. For seven years he stored food.

When the bad years came, people from all over Egypt came to Joseph for food. There was enough food to feed Egypt as well as people from other lands. One day, some men from Canaan, who had come to buy grain, bowed before Joseph. Joseph recognized them as his brothers. When they realized who Joseph was, the brothers begged for his forgiveness and felt ashamed for what they had done to him. Joseph forgave them.

Challenge:

Help Jacob find the pieces of fabric to make Joseph a coat.

SS2846

Jochebed and Miriam

Exodus 1:1-2:10; Numbers 26:59

A new king came into power in Egypt. Pharaoh said to his people, "...the Israelites have become much too numerous for us. Come, we must deal shrewdly with them...." He put slave masters over them and forced hard labor on them. He was afraid the Israelites might turn against Egypt some day, fight against them, and leave the country. He gave orders to his people to throw every newborn Israelite baby boy into the Nile River to drown.

An Israelite woman named Jochebed gave birth to a son. She hid him for three months. When she could no longer hide him, she made a papyrus basket for him and coated it with tar and pitch to make it waterproof. Then she placed him in the basket and put him among the reeds along the banks of the Nile. Jochebed had her daughter, Miriam, watch over him.

Soon Pharaoh's daughter came to the Nile to bathe. She saw the basket among the reeds and sent her slave girl to get it. When she saw the baby, she felt sorry for him. Miriam came out of her hiding place and said to Pharaoh's daughter, "Shall I go and get one of the Hebrew women to nurse the baby for you?" "Yes, go," she told Miriam. The girl ran and got her mother. Pharoah's daughter said to Jochebed, "Take this baby and nurse him for me, and I will pay you." The baby's own mother took the baby and cared for him until he grew older. Then she took him to Pharaoh's daughter, and he became her son. "She named him Moses, saying, 'I drew him out of the water.' "

Challenge:

Help find baby Moses in the reeds.

Shining Star Publications, Copyright © 1992, A division of Good Apple

SS2846

19

SS2846

Moses

Exodus 2:11-3:22; 12:30-42; 13:20-14:31

Moses grew up in Pharaoh's palace, but he never forgot his people. He knew they were mistreated by the Egyptians, and unhappy. One day he killed an Egyptian he saw beating an Israelite. When his crime was discovered, Moses had to leave the country and hide in Midian, where he became a shepherd.

One day, he saw a bush on fire, but the flames did not burn it up! A voice called to Moses from the bush. "Take off your sandals, for the place where you are standing is holy ground." It was the voice of God. God told him to go back to Egypt to ask Pharaoh to free the Israelites. Moses and his brother Aaron went to Egypt. Pharaoh became angry when Moses and Aaron asked him to let the Israelites go. Pharaoh said he would never let them go. God punished Pharaoh and his people in many ways, until one night Pharaoh summoned Moses and Aaron. He said, "Up! Leave my people, you and the Israelites! Go, worship the Lord as you have requested. Take your flocks and herds, as you have said, and go. And also bless me." The Israelites had been in Egypt for 430 years. Moses began leading them across the desert. "By day the Lord went ahead of them in a pillar of cloud to guide them on their way and by night in a pillar of fire to give them light, so that they could travel by day or night."

The Egyptians were angry that they no longer had slaves to do their work. Pharaoh took his army and six hundred of the best chariots, along with all the other chariots of Egypt to pursue the Israelites and bring them back. Moses and his people came to the Red Sea. The people were terrified. Moses told them, "Do not be afraid. Stand firm and you will see the deliverance the Lord will bring you today." God told Moses, "...Raise your staff and stretch out your hand over the sea to divide the water so that the Israelites can go through the sea on dry ground...." Moses did as he was told. The Lord sent a mighty wind and rolled back the sea. Moses and his people crossed on dry land. They saw Pharaoh's army following them. Then the Lord said to Moses, "Stretch out your hand over the sea so that the waters may flow back over the Egyptians and their chariots and horsemen." When Moses did, "The water flowed back and covered the chariots and horsemen—the entire army of Pharaoh that had followed the Israelites into the sea. Not one of them survived."

"When the Israelites saw the great power the Lord displayed against the Egyptians, the people feared the Lord and put their trust in Him and in Moses His servant."

Challenge:

Moses' outstretched hands and staff divided the water. Find the path in the water so the Israelites can pass through on dry ground.

SS2846

Joshua

Joshua 1:1-5; 2:1-16, 24; 3:1-17; 4:1-18; 6:1-27

After the death of Moses, the Lord commanded Joshua to lead his people to the Promised Land. Joshua sent two of his men into the land to secretly find out more about it, especially the city of Jericho. The two men stayed in the house of Rahab. When the king of Jericho heard about the spies, he sent his men to get them, but Rahab had taken the two men and hidden them on the roof. She told the king's men, "Yes, the men came to me, but I did not know where they had come from. At dusk, when it was time to close the city gate, the men left." After the king's men were gone, Rahab said to the Israelites,"...please swear to me by the Lord that you will show kindness to my family, because I have shown kindness to you." The men assured her they would. She let them down the wall by a rope through her window, and told them how to escape the king's men.

When the two men returned to camp, they told Joshua, "The Lord has surely given the whole land into our hands; all the people are melting in fear because of us."

Early the next morning, Joshua led his people to the Jordan River to cross over into the Promised Land. The Lord told him to have the priests carry the ark of the covenant into the river. As soon as the priests with the ark set foot in the Jordan River, its waters from upstream stopped flowing. All Israel passed over until the whole nation had crossed the river on dry ground. As soon as everyone had passed over, the Lord told Joshua to send twelve men from among the people to pick up twelve stones from the middle of the river, right where the priests were standing. Then the priests carrying the ark walked to the other side of the river while the people watched. As soon as the priests set foot on dry land, the river started to flow again.

When the people got to the walled city of Jericho, the Lord said to Joshua, "...March around the city once with all the armed men. Do this for six days. Have seven priests carry trumpets of rams' horns in front of the ark. On the seventh day, march around the city seven times, with the priests blowing the trumpets. When you hear them sound a long blast on the trumpets, have all the people give a loud shout; then the wall of the city will collapse and the people will go up, every man straight in." Joshua did exactly what God told him, and they took the city. Joshua told the two men who had spied out the city to get Rahab and her family. Then the Israelites burned the city and everything in it. "So the Lord was with Joshua, and his fame spread throughout the land."

Challenge:

Joshua and the people marched around the city of Jericho seven times. Can you find the path around the city?

SS2846

SS2846

Samson

Judges 13:1-5, 24; 16:4-31

"Again the Israelites did evil in the eyes of the Lord, so the Lord delivered them into the hands of the Philistines for forty years." The Lord sent an angel to an Israelite man and his wife. The angel said to her, "You are sterile and childless, but you are going to conceive and have a son…. He will begin the deliverance of Israel from the hands of the Philistines." The woman gave birth to a son and called him Samson.

When he grew up, Samson was a man of great strength. One day he met and fell in love with a woman named Delilah. The rulers of the Philistines went to Delilah and said to her, "See if you can lure him into showing you the secret of his great strength and how we can overpower him so we may tie him up and subdue him. Each one of us will give you eleven hundred shekels of silver." Delilah tried several times to trick Samson into telling his secret. Finally, she said to him, "How can you say, 'I love you,' when you won't confide in me? This is the third time you have made a fool of me and haven't told me the secret of your great strength." She kept nagging him until he told her, "…If my head were shaved, my strength would leave me, and I would become as weak as any other man." Delilah sent word to the Philistine rulers. After Samson fell asleep in her lap, she had a man shave off his hair. Then Delilah called out, "Samson, the Philistines are upon you!" He woke from his sleep and did not know that his strength was gone. Then the Philistines seized him, put out his eyes, and took him down to Gaza. "Binding him with bronze shackles, they set him to grinding in the prison. But the hair on his head began to grow again after it had been shaved."

One day the Philistines assembled to offer a sacrifice to their god. In their celebration, they decided to have Samson entertain them. They brought him from the prison, and they stood him among the pillars of their temple. The temple was crowded with men and women and all the Philistine rulers. Samson prayed to the Lord, "O Sovereign Lord, remember me. O God, please strengthen me just once more, and let me with one blow get revenge on the Philistines for my two eyes." Then Samson braced himself against the two pillars and said, "Let me die with the Philistines!" He pushed with all his might, and the temple came down on the rulers and everyone in it.

Challenge:

Help tricky Delilah find her way through Samson's seven cut braids to reach the reward of silver for betraying him.

Shining Star Publications, Copyright © 1992, A division of Good Apple

SS2846

25

SS2846

Ruth

Ruth 1:1-18, 2:1-13, 4:13-17

There was a famine in the land of Israel. Elimelech, his wife Naomi, and their two sons Mahlon and Kilion left Bethlehem to go to the country of Moab to live.

Years later, Elimelech died, and Noami was left with two sons. They fell in love and married Moabite women, Orpah and Ruth. Everything was fine for ten years; then Mahlon and Kilion died. Noami heard that the famine in Israel was over, and she longed to go back. Her two daughters-in-law, Orpah and Ruth, decided to go with her.

It was a long way back to Bethlehem, and Naomi felt that there was no reason for her daughters-in-law to return with her. She said to them, "Return home, my daughters. Why would you come with me? Am I going to have any more sons who could become your husbands?" The two girls wept. Orpah kissed her and went back home, but Ruth clung to her and said, "Where you go I will go, and where you stay I will stay. Your people will be my people and your God my God." Naomi realized that Ruth was determined to go with her.

They arrived in Bethlehem about harvest time. Ruth went to work in a field, picking up grain left by the harvesters. The owner of the field was Boaz, who was related to Elimelech. When Boaz went to his fields, he saw Ruth working and asked his foreman about her. He told Boaz that she was from Moab and she returned with Naomi after her husband had died. Boaz said to Ruth, "I've been told all about what you have done for your mother-in-law since the death of your husband—how you left your father and mother and your homeland and came to live with a people you did not know before. May the Lord repay you for what you have done." Ruth replied, "May I continue to find favor in your eyes, my lord."

Later, Boaz married Ruth. They had a son named Obed. Obed would become the father of Jesse, the father of David.

Challenge:

Ruth worked hard picking up grain left over from the harvest. Help Boaz find Ruth in the field.

SS2846

27

Hannah

1 Samuel 1

A man named Elkanah and his wife Hannah had no children. They went to the temple to pray every year. Hannah would pray for a child, but no child was born. One day when she went to the temple, she meet Eli the priest. She prayed for God to give her a baby. She promised that if He gave her a son, she would give him back to do God's work. Eli the priest went up to Hannah and said, "Go in peace, and may the God of Israel grant you what you have asked of him."

Soon God gave Hannah a son, and she named him Samuel. She did not forget the promise she had made to God. When Samuel was five years old, she took him to the temple to give him back to God. Hannah said to Eli the priest, "As surely as you live, my lord, I am the woman who stood here beside you praying to the Lord. I prayed for this child, and the Lord has granted me what I asked of him. So now I give him to the Lord. For his whole life he will be given over to the Lord." She left Samuel in the temple to minister before the Lord under Eli the priest, who looked after the boy as his own.

Challenge:

Help Hannah keep her promise to God. Help her find her way to the temple.

SS2846

Samuel

1 Samuel 3:1-19; 4:12-18; 8:1-22; 10:1

Samuel began ministering to the Lord in the temple when he was just a small child. One night, Samuel heard the Lord speak. Eli the priest told Samuel, "Go and lie down, and if he calls you, say, 'Speak, Lord, for your servant is listening.' " Samuel obeyed, and the Lord spoke to him. "The Lord was with Samuel as he grew up, and he let none of his words fall to the ground."

Years later when Eli was old, his two sons died during the Philistine capture of the ark. When Eli heard of their deaths and the capture of the ark, he fell over and died.

Samuel was a judge over Israel all the days of his life. When he grew old, he appointed his two sons, Joel and Abijah, judges for Israel. His sons did not live the way Samuel did; they were dishonest. The elders of Israel did not like this. They went to Samuel and said, "You are old, and your sons do not walk in your ways; now appoint a king to lead us, such as all the other nations have." Samuel prayed, and the Lord told him to warn the people what a king would do to them. Samuel told them, "When that day comes, you will cry out for relief from the king you have chosen, and the Lord will not answer you in that day." But the people refused to listen. They wanted a king, so God chose a man named Saul, and Samuel anointed him king over Israel.

Challenge:

Help Samuel find a king.

Shining Star Publications, Copyright © 1992, A division of Good Apple

SS2846

David

1 Samuel 17

The Philistines gathered their forces for war against Israel. They occupied one hill and the Israelites occupied another, with a valley between them. A giant named Goliath, from Gath, came out and shouted at the Israelite army, "Choose a man and have him come down to me. If he is able to fight and kill me, we will become your subjects; but if I overcome him and kill him, you will become our subjects and serve us." Every morning and evening for forty days, Goliath came forward and took his stand. All the Israelites were terrified; no one was willing to go against the giant.

An Israelite named Jesse had eight sons. Three of the oldest sons followed King Saul to war. The youngest son, David, stayed home and tended sheep for his father. One day Jesse sent David to the army camp to take food to his brothers. When David reached the camp, he ran up to the battle line to greet his brothers. As he was talking with them, Goliath stepped out and shouted his challenge. When the Israelites saw Goliath, they ran in fear. David asked the men standing near him, "What will be done for the man who kills this Philistine...?" He was told that the reward was great wealth and Saul's daughter in marriage! David went to Saul and said, "Let no one lose heart on account of this Philistine; your servant will go and fight him." Saul replied, "...you are only a boy, and he has been a fighting man from his youth." David said, "Your servant has been keeping his father's sheep. When a lion or a bear came and carried off a sheep from the flock, I went after it, struck it, and rescued the sheep from its mouth." Saul said to David, "Go, and the Lord be with you."

He gave David his armor, but David took it off. David took only his staff, sling, and five smooth stones from a stream, which he put in the pouch of his shepherd's bag. Then he went to face Goliath. When Goliath saw that David was only a boy, he mocked him and said, "...I'll give your flesh to the birds of the air and the beasts of the field!" David said to the giant, "You come against me with sword and spear and javelin, but I come against you in the name of the Lord Almighty, the God of the armies of Israel, whom you have defied. This day the Lord will hand you over to me, and I'll strike you down...." David reached in his bag and took out a stone. He put it in his sling and threw it at the giant. It struck the Philistine on the forehead, and he fell facedown on the ground. David ran and stood over him. When the Israelite army saw this, they began chasing the Philistines and defeated them.

Several years later, God made David king of Israel.

Challenge:

Help David find five smooth stones from the stream and then find Goliath.

SS2846

Solomon

1 Kings 1:28-40; 2:1-4; 3:1-15; 5:1-12; 6:19, 38; 8:6-9

King David, the ruler of Israel, had a son named Solomon. When David was near death, he made Solomon king. David said to his son, "Be strong, show yourself a man, and observe what the lord your God requires: Walk in his ways, and keep his decrees and commands, his laws and requirements, as written in the Law of Moses, so that you may prosper in all you do and wherever you go...." Solomon loved peace, and while he was king, there were no wars. Like his father, he wanted to build a temple, so Solomon made up his mind to build the temple in praise of God, for all the good things God had given him.

He made an alliance with Pharaoh, king of Egypt, and married his daughter. Solomon brought her back to the City of David until he finished building his palace and the temple of the Lord.

One night Solomon had a dream. The Lord appeared to him and said, "Ask for whatever you want me to give you." Solomon answered, "...So give your servant a discerning heart to govern your people and to distinguish between right and wrong." God was pleased to hear this. He replied, "Since you have asked for this and not for long life or wealth for yourself, nor have asked for the death of your enemies but for discernment in administering justice, I will do what you have asked. I will give you a wise and discerning heart, so that there will never have been anyone like you, nor will there ever be. Moreover, I will give you what you have not asked for—both riches and honor— so that in your lifetime you will have no equal among kings. And if you walk in my ways and obey my statutes and commands as David your father did, I will give you a long life." Then Solomon woke up. He returned to Jerusalem and sacrificed burnt offerings in front of the ark of the Lord's covenant.

Solomon wanted the temple to be built of cedar, but no cedar grew in Israel. He wrote a letter to King Hiram of Tyre, who had been a friend of David, Solomon's father. Solomon and Hiram made a treaty: Hiram would supply Solomon with all the cedar he needed, and Solomon would send Hiram wheat and olive oil.

It took seven years to build the temple. Solomon had it lined inside and outside with gold. Only the best was good enough for God. Solomon placed inside the temple the ark of the covenant of the Lord, which contained the Ten Commandments written on stone that God had given to Moses. This temple in Jerusalem was a wonderful place of worship for all Israel.

Challenge:

Solomon wanted the temple to be built of cedar, but no cedar grew in Israel. Help Solomon's letter reach his friend King Hiram of Tyre.

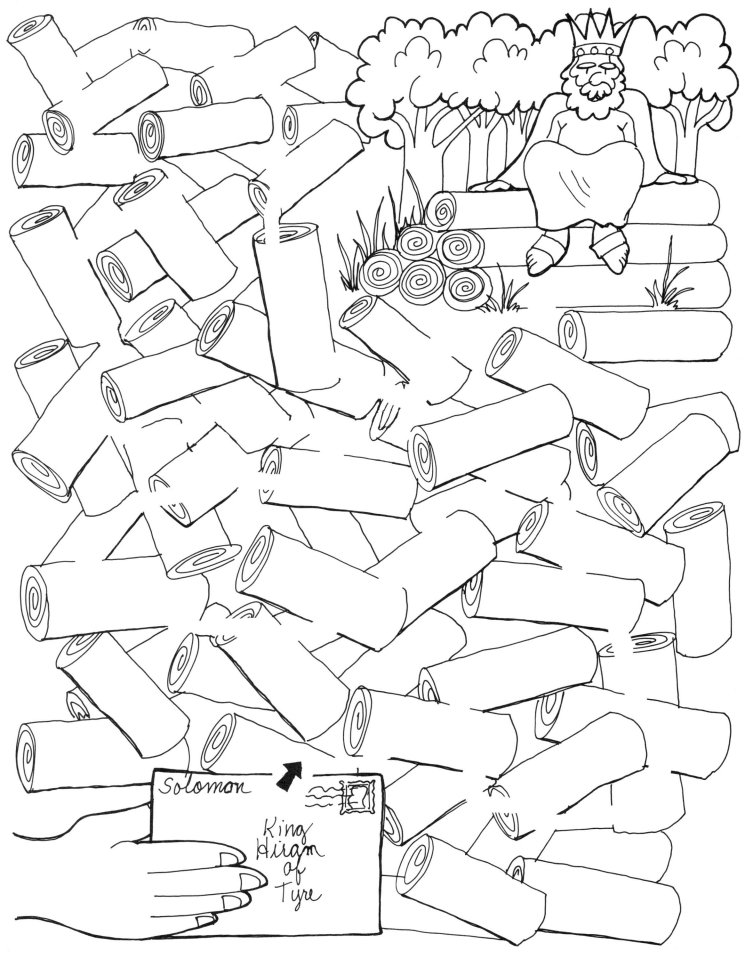

SS2846

Elijah

1 Kings 17:1-4; 18:17-46

God sent his prophet Elijah to warn wicked King Ahab that a drought was coming to Israel. For three and a half years no rain fell on Israel. The crops dried up, animals died, and the people suffered. Finally God sent Elijah back to wicked King Ahab with another message.

He said to the King, "I have not made trouble for Israel, but you and your father's family have. You have abandoned the Lord's commands and have followed the Baals. Now summon the people from all over Israel to meet me on Mount Carmel. And bring the four hundred and fifty prophets of Baal and the four hundred prophets of Asherah, who eat at Jezebel's table."

Ahab spread the word. When the meeting on Mount Carmel began, Elijah said to the prophets and the people of Israel, "I am the only one of the Lord's prophets left, but Baal has four hundred and fifty prophets. Get two bulls for us. Let them choose one for themselves, and let them cut it into pieces and put it on the wood but not set fire to it. I will prepare the other bull and put it on the wood but not set fire to it. Then you call on the name of your god, and I will call on the name of the Lord. The god who answers by fire—he is God." They all agreed that it was a good plan.

Elijah had the prophets of Baal choose a bull and prepare it first. They called on Baal from morning till late afternoon, but there was no answer. Then Elijah said to the people, "Come here to me." They watched him as he took twelve stones, one for each of the tribes descended from Jacob. With the stones, he made an altar and dug a trench around it. Then he arranged the wood, cut the bull into pieces, and laid it on the wood. He said, "Fill four large jars with water and pour it on the offering and on the wood." Elijah had the people do this three times, until the water filled the trench. Then he prayed, "O Lord, God of Abraham, Isaac and Israel, let it be known today that you are God in Israel and that I am your servant and have done all these things at your command. Answer me, O Lord, answer me, so these people will know that you, O Lord, are God, and that you are turning their hearts back again." Then the fire of the Lord fell and burned up the altar and everything on it! When the people saw this, they fell down and cried, "The Lord—he is God! The Lord—he is God!" Soon, rain fell on Israel, and the drought was ended.

Challenge:

Find a path to each of the twelve stones Elijah will use to build an altar.

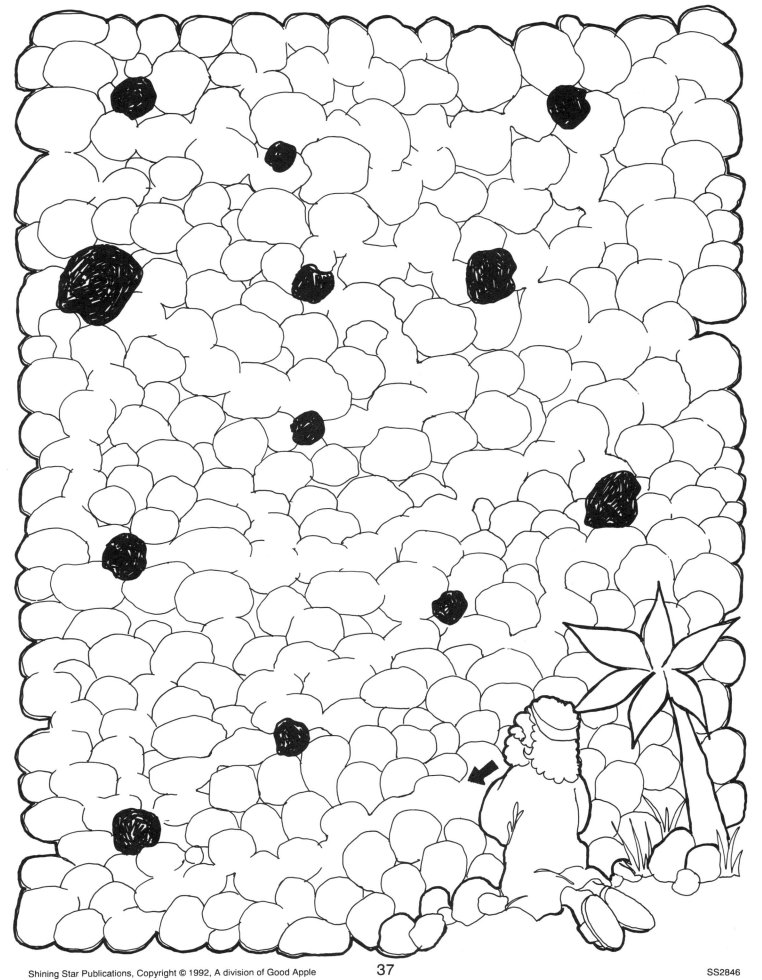

Shadrach, Meshach and Abednego

Daniel 3

King Nebuchadnezzar made a huge image of gold and commanded everyone to fall down and worship it when they heard the sound of music. Anyone that did not obey would immediately be thrown into a blazing furnace. Some astrologers came forward and said to the king, "There are some Jews whom you have set over the affairs of the province of Babylon—Shadrach, Meshach and Abednego—who pay no attention to you, O king. They neither serve your gods nor worship the image of gold you have set up."

King Nebuchadnezzar was outraged and summoned the three men. When Shadrach, Meshach, and Abednego were brought before the king, he said, "Is it true,… that you do not serve my gods or worship the image of gold I have set up?" The men replied, "O Nebuchadnezzar, we do not need to defend ourselves before you in this matter. If we are thrown into the blazing furnace, the God we serve is able to save us from it, and He will rescue us from your hand, O king."

The king was furious. He ordered the furnace to be heated seven times hotter than usual. Then soldiers tied up Shadrach, Meshach and Abednego and threw them into the blazing furnace. The flames were so hot, the heat killed the soldiers that put the three men into the furnace. Nebuchadnezar stared in amazement! "Look!" he said. "I see four men walking around in the fire, unbound and unharmed, and the fourth looks like a son of the gods." The king shouted, "Shadrach, Meshach and Abednego, servants of the Most High God, come out! Come here!" They came out of the fire, unharmed. Nebuchadnezzar said, "Praise be to the God of Shadrach, Meshach and Abednego, who has sent his angel and rescued his servants! They trusted in him and defied the king's command and were willing to give up their lives rather than serve or worship any god except their own God."

Challenge:

The king shouted, "Shadrach, Meshach and Abednego, servants of the Most High God, come out! Come here!" Find a path for the three men to pass through the fire to King Nebuchadnezzar.

SS2846

Shining Star Publications, Copyright © 1992, A division of Good Apple

SS2846

Daniel

Daniel 6:1-23

King Darius liked Daniel. He was capable, honest, and trustworthy. The king planned to place Daniel over the whole kingdom. This made the king's other officers angry, and they tried to find charges against Daniel to get rid of him. They couldn't find anything, so they persuaded the king to make a decree that anyone who prayed to any god for thirty days, except to King Darius, would be thrown into a lions' den.

When Daniel heard of this decree, he went home and prayed as usual in his upstairs room where the windows faced Jerusalem. Three times every day Daniel got down on his knees and prayed, giving thanks to his God, as he always did. When the king's administrators saw Daniel praying, they went to the king and said, "Did you not publish a decree that during the next thirty days anyone who prays to any god or man except to you, O king, would be thrown into the lions' den?" When the king heard that Daniel had broken his decree, he was greatly distressed. He was determined to rescue Daniel, but could not. As Daniel was thrown into the lions' den, the king said to him, "May your God, whom you serve continually, rescue you!" Then they rolled the stone in front of the den, and the king sealed it with his signet ring. The king was so worried that night, he did not eat or sleep.

At the first light of dawn, he got up and hurried to the lions' den. The king called out, "Daniel, servant of the living God, has your God, whom you serve continually, been able to rescue you from the lions?" Daniel answered, "O king, live forever! My God sent his angel, and he shut the mouths of the lions. They have not hurt me, because I was found innocent in his sight. Nor have I ever done any wrong before you, O king." The king was overjoyed, and Daniel was lifted from the den. No wound was found on him, because Daniel trusted God.

Challenge:

Help the soldiers put Daniel in the lions' den. Draw a line that shows how they must go.

SS2846

Jonah

Jonah 1:1-3:3

The Lord told Jonah to go to Nineveh, but Jonah ran away. He thought he could hide from the Lord on board a ship. The Lord knew where Jonah was. He sent a great storm which made all the sailors afraid. They threw their cargo into the sea to lighten the ship. They thought they were going to drown. The sailors said to each other, "Come, let us cast lots to find out who is responsible for this calamity." Jonah lost. They asked him, "...who is responsible for making all this trouble for us? What do you do? Where do you come from? What is your country? From what people are you?"

Jonah answered, "I am a Hebrew and I worship the Lord, the God of heaven, who made the sea and the land." Jonah told them, "Pick me up and throw me into the sea, and it will become calm. I know that it is my fault that this great storm has come upon you." Instead, the sailors tried to row back to shore, but they could not. The sea grew even wilder, and they cried, "O Lord, please do not let us die for taking this man's life. Do not hold us accountable for killing an innocent man, for you, O Lord, have done as you pleased." Then they took Jonah and threw him overboard, and the sea calmed down.

Jonah didn't drown! The Lord had a great fish swallow him. Jonah was inside the fish for three days and three nights. While in the fish, Jonah prayed. He asked God to forgive him and thanked God for saving his life. Then the Lord commanded the fish to spit Jonah out on dry land.

The Lord came to Jonah a second time and said, "Go to the great city of Nineveh and proclaim to it the message I give you." Jonah obeyed the Lord.

Challenge:

Help the big fish find Jonah, so Jonah won't drown.

Answer Key

Page 5

Page 7

Page 9

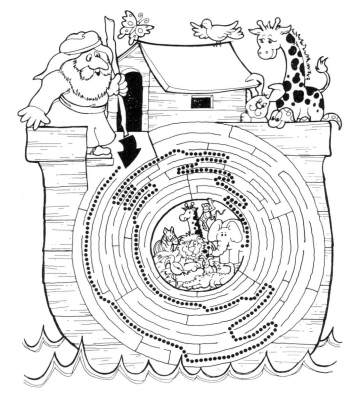

Page 11

The Promised Land

SS2846

Page 13

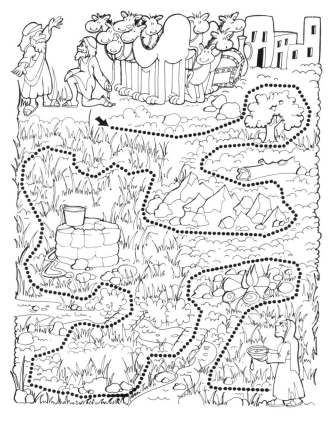

Page 15

Rachel

Leah

stairs

food

clothes

Page 17

Page 19

Page 21

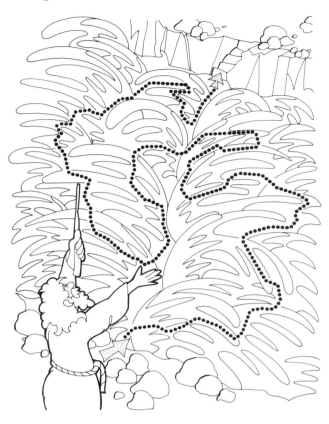

Page 23

Page 25

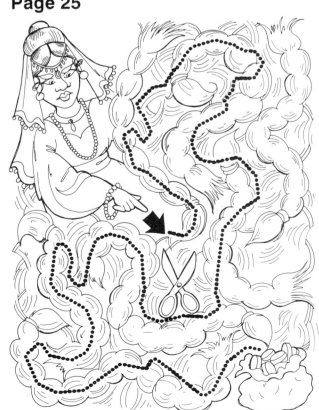

Page 27

SS2846

Page 29

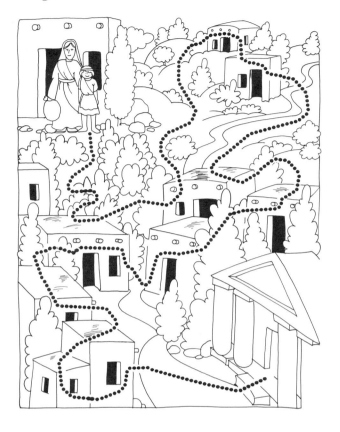

Page 31

Page 33

Page 35

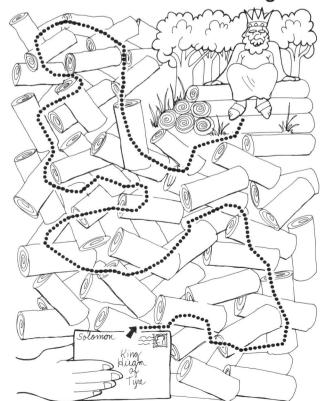

SS2846

Page 37

Page 39

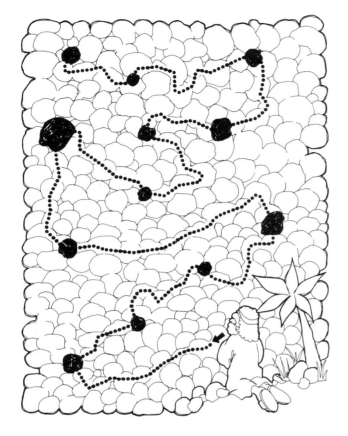

Page 41

Page 43

SS2846